Mummies, Bones, & Body Parts

CHARLOTTE WILCOX

CAROLRHODA BOOKS, INC./MINNEAPOLIS

Front cover: *A young girl from the Inca empire of Peru, who was sacrificed on a mountaintop five hundred years ago, stares across time.*
Back cover: *The mummy of the Egyptian king Seti I*
Page one: *A human skull, pierced by an arrow, tells a story of a violent end.*
Page two: *From piles of bones and other remains, like these found in Peru, scientists piece together clues about how people lived and died in the past.*
Opposite page: *The dead tell many tales. These people lived in Chile, where the dry heat of the desert preserved their bodies.*

Carolrhoda Books, Inc.
A division of Lerner Publishing Group
241 First Avenue North
Minneapolis, MN 55401 U.S.A.

Website address: www.lernerbooks.com

LIBRARY OF CONGRESS CATALOGING-IN-PUBLICATION DATA

Wilcox, Charlotte.
Mummies, bones, & body parts / Charlotte Wilcox.
p. cm.
Includes bibliographical references and index.
Summary: Describes the wide variety of human remains, the use and abuse of them, what they reveal about life in the past, and contemporary attitudes toward the dead.
ISBN 1-57505-428-0 (lib. bdg.: alk. paper)
ISBN 1-57505-486-8 (pbk.: alk. paper)
1. Mummies—Juvenile literature. 2. Human remains (Archaeology)—Juvenile literature. 3. Funeral rites and ceremonies—Juvenile literature. I. Title.
GN293 .W56 2000
559.97—dc21   99-050516

Manufactured in the United States of America
1 2 3 4 5 6 – JR – 05 04 03 02 01 00

CONTENTS

A Pazyryk Lady's Tomb

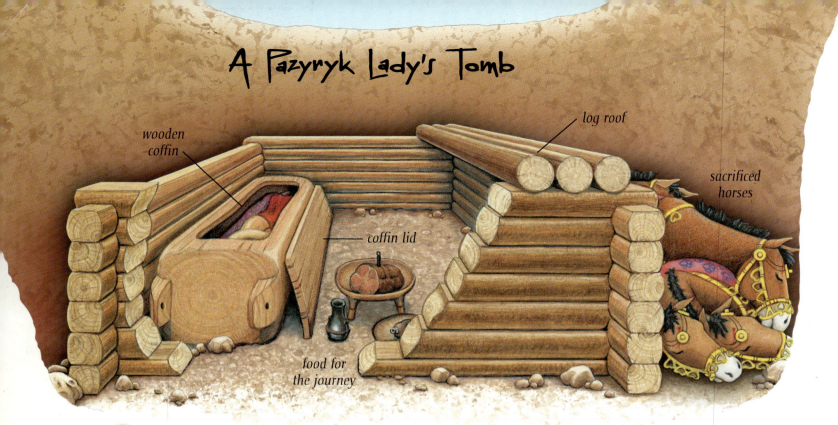

wooden coffin

log roof

coffin lid

food for the journey

sacrificed horses

Chapter 1

THE LONG REST

A lovely young lady died about 2,400 years ago. She was a noblewoman from a tribe called the Pazyryk. They raised horses and sheep in the mountains where Russia, China, and Mongolia meet.

The woman was only about twenty-five years old when she died. But she held an important position in her community. Her death brought sadness to the whole tribe. The Pazyryk believed the young woman's soul would travel to a beautiful mountain grassland far away. But her body was still with them. They worked together to care for it.

The Pazyryk people of Asia believed the souls of the dead could travel to another land. They treated the dead with great respect and care. The log-lined tomb (cross section opposite page and left) of a Pazyryk woman who died some 2,400 years ago contained everything, including good riding horses, that the woman would need on her journey to another life.

PREPARING FOR BURIAL

The woman died in winter, when it was impossible to dig a grave in the frozen ground. Her relatives had to keep her body until spring. They cut out the softest parts (organs and muscles) because these would decay the fastest. They filled the body with fur and spices. They dressed the lady in her best clothes—striped wool skirt, silk top, braided belt, and high riding boots. They fixed her hair with a three-foot-high, gold-covered hairpiece. Then they wrapped her in a fur blanket.

Men from the tribe traveled fifteen miles on horseback to the forest. They cut down a tree to build the coffin. It had to be nearly eight feet long because of the woman's tall hairpiece. When the ground was soft, the men dug a gigantic hole in the earth. In the bottom, they built a room with log walls.

7

THE FUNERAL

By late June, everything was ready for the funeral. The body was carefully laid in the coffin. The woman's family placed some of her belongings inside—a mirror, dishes, and beads. Then they nailed the lid shut and lowered the coffin into the deep grave.

Finally, the woman's most valuable treasures were buried with her—six horses, all dressed in gold-covered harnesses. The Pazyryk needed good horses to live in the mountains. They believed the lady would also need horses after death. The horses were led to the edge of the hole. A man hit each horse very hard in the forehead with an ax. Then the horses were lowered into the hole.

A roof of logs was placed over the burial room. All the dirt was pushed back into the hole. Then it was covered with a pile of rocks several feet high. The woman's relatives were satisfied that they had given her a safe place to start her journey to another life. They thought her body would rest in peace.

Some of the earliest tattoos ever recorded cover the noblewoman's body.

Not long after the funeral, rain or melted snow filled the burial room. It soon froze, sealing the coffin in a block of ice. A few years later, another tribe uncovered the grave and buried a man in it. The woman was not disturbed. Her body remained safe in the ice-filled grave. Some time later, robbers dug into the grave. But once again the woman was not disturbed.

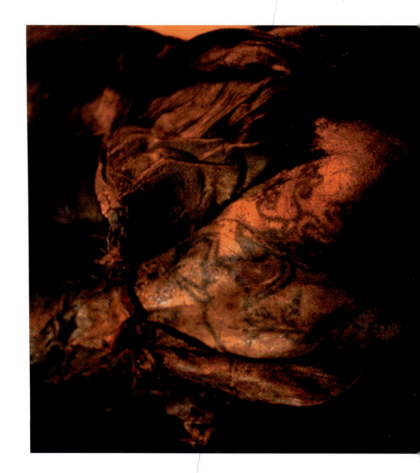

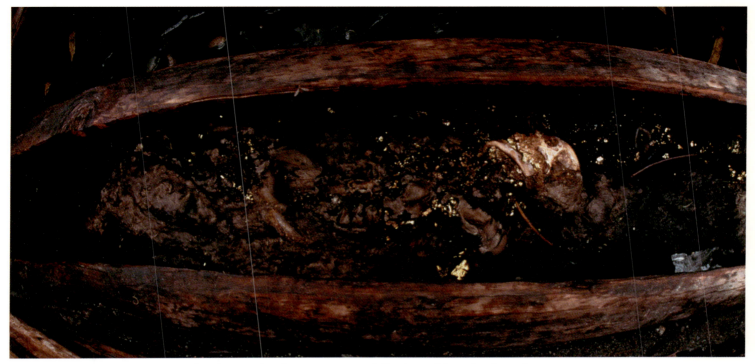

The woman's tomb, frozen in ice for thousands of years, was carefully thawed by scientists who discovered it in 1993.

A MUMMY IS FOUND

In 1993, Russian scientist Natalia Polosmak brought a team of researchers to the mountains. They wanted to learn more about the Pazyryk people. Under hundreds of pounds of dirt and rocks, they found a grave. In the bottom was the woman's coffin still sealed with nails pounded in by her relatives.

After days of slowly melting the ice, scientists uncovered the woman's body. Her once beautiful face was mostly bones, but the rest of her body was well preserved. The scientists had mixed feelings about what they were doing. Some even had nightmares. After taking the body away for study, they sent it back to a museum near the mountain where the woman had lived and died. She is close to the place where her family buried her, but far from the peaceful rest they tried to provide.

A graveyard is a place where the bodies of the dead are put to rest. Graveyards are frightening places to some people, sacred to others, and sad places to most everyone.

Chapter 2

LOOKING AFTER THE DEAD

When people die, they leave their bodies behind. The living are left to care for the dead. Caring for the dead has been an important part of human life throughout history.

Seeing the body of a loved one decay is disturbing. For this reason, bodies are usually placed out of sight fairly soon after death. Some societies place their dead high in special trees where no one is allowed to look. Others send dead bodies far out to sea in funeral boats. Some bodies are cremated, or burned to ashes.

The most common way of caring for the dead all over the world is burial. Everyone knows the body will decay, but no one sees it. For thousands of years, human bodies have been buried in the ground, in caves, or in special burial houses. Scientists can only guess how many billions of people have been buried on our planet.

Ways of caring for the dead are as varied as the people of the earth. The Crow Indians of North America traditionally placed their dead on platforms high in tree branches.

Most bodies that are buried begin to decay very soon. Decay is caused by bacteria and fungi that grow in the dead body and eat the tissues, beginning just a few hours after death. Within a day or two, decay causes the body to change color and give off an odor. After a few weeks, the softest parts of the body begin to be eaten away. Within a few years, all the soft tissue (skin, muscles, and organs) is completely eaten up, with only bones left behind.

STOPPING DECAY

In some cultures, dead bodies are embalmed before burial. Embalming preserves the dead body from decay, sometimes for only a short time, sometimes for many centuries. People all over the world have embalmed the dead for thousands of years. In modern North America, most embalming is intended to last only a few days, until the funeral takes place. Then the body is buried and begins to decay.

Some ancient cultures used embalming to preserve dead bodies from *ever* decaying. In places like Egypt and the Inca empire of South America, they were very successful. Millions of bodies have been preserved for thousands of years in those regions. Preserved bodies are called mummies.

Many mummified bodies have been found in Egypt, a place where embalming and burial were highly developed in ancient times.

WHAT MAKES A MUMMY?

In a mummy, some or all of the soft tissue does not decay after death. This happens when the bacteria and fungi that cause decay cannot grow in the dead body. Some mummies are preserved from decay by embalming. Others are preserved by natural conditions where the body is placed.

Mummification happens most often when the body dries out quickly after death, because bacteria and fungi need water to live. A body placed in the sun or in hot, dry sand may turn into a mummy. A body embalmed with chemicals, fire, or smoke (removing all water from the tissues soon after death) may become a mummy too.

Mummification also happens when a body is quickly and permanently frozen soon after death, because most bacteria cannot grow in below-freezing temperatures. Some mummies are buried in soil containing chemicals that kill bacteria, or in caves that contain gases that kill bacteria. A body will also become a mummy if all air is taken away from it, since bacteria and fungi need air as well as water to grow. Bodies sealed in airtight coffins have been preserved in this way.

Not all mummies are created on purpose. Some just happen. This person's body dried out quickly and thoroughly in the hot desert air of Chile, creating mummified remains.

New Ways to Make Mummies

Modern scientists have developed new ways to preserve bodies, creating modern mummies. One method is called cryonics. Cryonics is the practice of freezing a body in hopes of bringing the person back to life in the future. Usually the goal is to freeze the body until a cure is found for the disease that caused the person's death.

Bodies preserved in this way must be specially treated right after death. Blood must be removed and replaced with a special substance similar to what is used to preserve organs for transplantation. The body is then frozen at an extremely low temperature—lower than three hundred degrees Fahrenheit below zero. This is done by placing the body in a large container filled with liquid nitrogen.

The first person ever to be preserved by cryonics was James Bedford, who died of cancer in 1967. His frozen body is stored at a cryonics facility near Phoenix, Arizona. Many other people since then have had their bodies frozen at death.

No one knows if they will ever be revived. Scientists have only been successful in reviving animals frozen for just a few hours. Even so, people and their families continue to spend $30,000 to $120,000 for cryonic storage. They have the same hopes the ancient Egyptians had, that preserving the body will allow them to walk and talk with their loved ones again someday.

Hoping that scientists will someday be able to reverse death and cure all diseases, some people have chosen to have their remains or the remains of loved ones placed in cryonic storage. Two members of the same family are preserved in this container in Arizona.

The hardest part of the human body to destroy, bones are also the most common form of human remains available for study.

THE BITS WE LEAVE BEHIND

Most bodies don't become mummies. But they still leave evidence behind. Bacteria and fungi cannot eat bone. The skeleton is the longest-lasting part of the body. Human bones have survived being burned, cut in pieces, crushed, and dissolved with chemicals. Bones can last for centuries after the bodies they once wore have completely disappeared.

Anything that is left of a human body is called the remains. This can be an entire preserved body, body parts, bones, or ashes. Bones are the most common form of human remains. Skeletons, bones, and bone fragments are found anyplace in the world where humans have died.

Most people expect that, after burial, their bodies will remain unseen and untouched. But this does not always happen. Bodies and bones are unearthed for many reasons. Scientists find bodies while looking for human remains to study. Grave robbers hunting for treasures to sell may dig bodies up in ancient burial grounds. Other bodies are dug up accidentally, when people build new roads or plow new fields.

Paleopathologists sometimes study teeth and bones as well as soft tissues for clues about health, diet, and nutrition in the past.

STUDYING HUMAN REMAINS

Whenever a human body, body part, or bone is found, someone has to study it. Did the person die by accident or has a crime been committed? When did the person die and who was he or she? Many different kinds of scientists work to draw the answers out of bodies and bones.

Forensic anthropologists study recent human remains to solve crimes or settle disputes in court. Even tiny fragments of human tissue, hair, or bone can give them important clues.

Physical anthropologists study ancient human remains, most often skeletons and bones. If the body is ancient, an archaeologist may also be called in to examine the place where the body was found. Archaeologists investigate the past by studying artifacts (such as clothing, tools, and artworks), buildings, ancient writing, and other objects.

Paleopathologists also examine ancient human remains, especially the preserved soft tissues of mummies. Paleopathologists study diseases, health, and nutrition of the past. They use some of the same methods modern doctors use on living people to answer questions about how humans lived long, long ago.

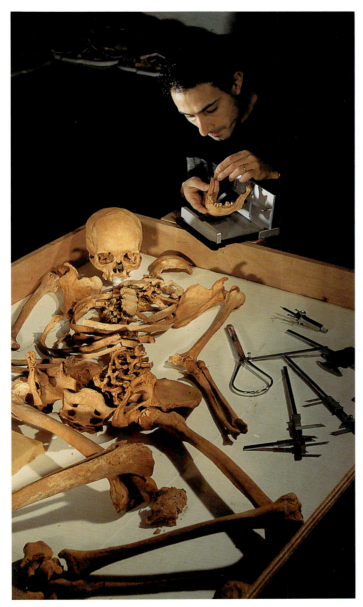

These scientists study human history from different angles. Without human remains to study, forensic anthropologists, physical anthropologists, and paleopathologists would be unable to do their jobs. Bodies or skeletons—sometimes even small pieces of them—can tell scientists whether people were male or female and how old they were at death. Human remains hold clues about how people lived and how they died.

Many of the photographs in this book show human remains. Some are disturbing or even shocking. Most are of specimens that are already on display in a museum or school. Many of the photographs point out the importance of human remains to science and education. But human remains are often handled or kept in disrespectful ways. A few of the photographs in this book are included to show how *not* to treat the dead. In all cases, these mummies, bones, and body parts should be viewed with respect.

Archaeologists study ancient people, their cultures and their artifacts. Here an archaeologist uncovers the coffin of an Egyptian mummy.

The age of this well-preserved body, found in a peat bog in Ireland in the late 1970s, remains a mystery to scientists.

3 Chapter

HOW OLD ARE THEY?

One of the first things scientists try to find out about remains is how old they are. Did the person die recently or a long time ago? Scientists look at three things to decide how old human remains are: the location of the remains, the things found with the body or bones, and the remains themselves.

THE WOMAN IN THE BOG

Nearly fifteen hundred preserved bodies have turned up in peat bogs in northern Europe over the years. Some may be up to three thousand years old. Acids in the soil of peat bogs keep bacteria from growing, turning bodies into mummies. Meenybraddan Woman is a mummified body found in a peat bog in Ireland in the late 1970s.

Investigators looked first at the area where Meenybraddan Woman was found for clues about her age. How deep was the body buried? What was on top of it and around it? What changes could be seen in the soil between the body and the surface? How long did it take for these changes to occur? The place where Meenybraddan Woman was found had been disturbed by people digging peat, so scientists used other tools to determine her age.

They studied items found with the body, such as clothing. When experts examined Meenybraddan Woman's woolen cloak, they found it was a style worn from the late 1500s to the late 1600s.

Scientists also studied Meenybraddan Woman's body for clues. Some of her preserved tissue was tested using radiocarbon dating. This is a way of finding the age of old material by measuring how much carbon it contains. Radiocarbon dating can only be done on something that was once alive, such as human or animal tissue, plant material, and artifacts made from plants, skins, bone, hair, or feathers. Meenybraddan Woman's body was radiocarbon dated to about A.D. 1200.

How old was the body? Studying the clothes gave one answer, while dating the tissue gave another. Both methods are considered good ways to date a body, but in the case of Meenybraddan Woman at least one of them must be wrong.

Radiocarbon dating measures the amount of a radioactive form of carbon (carbon 14) contained in human or other once living remains. Measuring how much carbon 14 is still in remains gives scientists a good guess at their age. Here, a lab worker prepares a sample for dating.

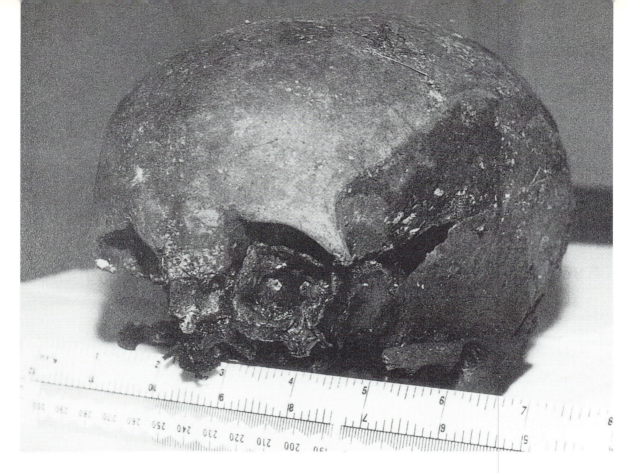

This skull, pulled from a peat bog in England, solved a crime but left many questions unanswered.

THE LINDOW MUMMY MURDER MYSTERY

Some scientists question the accuracy of radiocarbon dating. Mummies found in Lindow Moss, a peat bog near Cheshire, England, show why. Workers digging in the bog found a human head in 1983. They took it to the police. The police thought the head belonged to a local woman who had been missing since 1960. The woman's husband, who lived next to the bog, had always said he did not know what happened to his wife.

The police told the husband they now had his wife's head, pulled from the bog. The husband then confessed that he had killed his wife, cut her body into pieces, and buried it in the bog. He was sentenced to prison for murder.

Clues to the age of Lindow II were found in his mouth, where no evidence of fillings or other modern dental work could be found.

The husband said he buried all the body parts. But in spite of much digging, no more human remains were found. One police inspector had doubts about the head. So he ordered radiocarbon dating and was told the head was almost two thousand years old! That left the police with a confessed murderer, and no body at all. Scientists named the head Lindow I.

The case took a different turn the next summer. The same crew working in Lindow Moss found part of a right leg and foot. This time they called an archaeologist, Rick Turner. He began digging in the bog and found the complete top half of a body. The bottom half was missing, except for the lower right leg and foot the workers had found first.

Although Turner suspected the body was ancient, he asked the police to take a look. Some police investigators thought the body might belong to the murdered wife. The body came to be known as Lindow II.

The first hint that Lindow II was very old came from X rays. X rays showed not even one filling in the full set of teeth. This convinced Turner and other scientists that the body was not modern. Almost all modern bodies have some metal fillings in the teeth. But the police were not convinced.

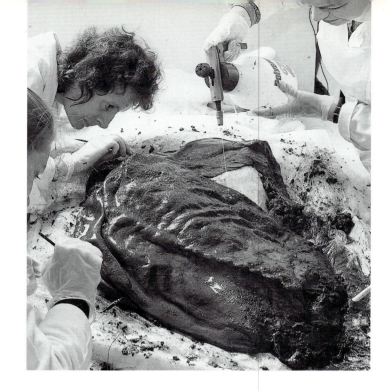

Scientists work together to preserve, clean, and study the remains of Lindow II. Newspaper reporters nicknamed the man "Pete Moss," after his burial place, the English peat bog known as Lindow Moss.

Turner had the body radiocarbon dated. The first report said Lindow II was at least 1,000 years old. Later the same laboratory dated the body at about 1,500 years. A second laboratory dated Lindow II at about 2,000 years old. Yet another laboratory showed the age to be about 1,650 years old. This led some police researchers to claim the radiocarbon tests could not be trusted.

Skeptical police looked once again at the head of Lindow I. They sent it to Peter Vanezis, a famous forensic pathologist. He studied features of the head and compared it to photos of the missing woman. Vanezis, who distrusts radiocarbon dating, believes the skull could be that of the murdered wife.

In 1987, more body parts turned up in Lindow Moss. This body was called Lindow III. It was accidentally cut in pieces by digging machinery. Even so, the entire body was recovered, except for the head. Did this body belong to the head known as Lindow I? At first, some scientists thought so. Later tests showed that the head belonged to a woman, while the remains known as Lindow III belonged to a man.

Almost a year and a half later more human remains were found. They included a right thigh and part of a left leg. Most scientists think these are not a separate body but the missing parts of Lindow II.

Were there two, three, or even four bodies in the bog? Are they one thousand years old, two thousand years old, or somewhere in between? Or is one a modern murder victim? New research methods may answer these questions in the future.

This hat, found with a mummified body in a glacier in Canada and carbon dated to be about 550 years old, looks surprisingly modern.

Canada's Iceman

In the summer of 1999, three hunters were hiking through a park reserve in northwest British Columbia, Canada, near where Alaska, British Columbia, and Yukon Territory meet. On the edge of a glacier, the hunters made a grisly discovery—a human body sticking out of the ice.

Because the body was found on land controlled by native peoples called the Champagne and Aishihik First Nations, a team of scientists and Indian leaders went to the park to investigate. They found the body still frozen and took it to a museum for preservation.

At the museum, clothing and artifacts found with the body were radiocarbon dated and found to be about 550 years old. Scientists agree that Canada's Iceman lived before Europeans came to the region, and scientists and First Nations people hope that further study of his body will yield clues about how life was lived long ago. Indians have named the area where the man was found Kwaday Dän Sinchi, which means "Long Ago Person Found."

Chapter 4

WHAT KILLED THEM ?

After determining the age of human remains, scientists often next look to see how a person died. Murder, disease, and accidents leave traces behind on skin, bone, and body parts. But those traces may be hard to see with the naked eye.

THE PAST UNDER A MICROSCOPE

Much of medical research is done under a microscope. Scientists usually place a thin slice of tissue on a glass slide. But most mummies are too dry and brittle to slice. Scientists must rehydrate the tissues so they can be studied. Rehydrating puts water back into the tissues. It is often done by soaking the tissues in human blood serum. This is the clear, thin, liquid part of blood.

Sometimes, the cause of death seems clear. This man died in about 3500 B.C., but not from the wound to his head. Instead, an arrow traveling through his breastbone pierced a major artery.

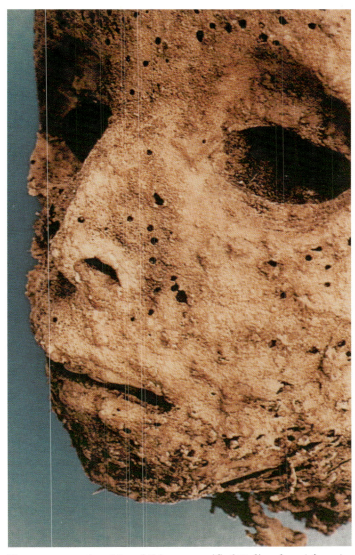

Tiny scars on the skin of this mummified Italian boy (above) led scientists to believe he died of smallpox. Tissue from mummies (above, right) is sometimes so dry that moisture, in the form of blood serum, must be added to it before it can be studied.

Researchers studied the body of a two-year-old boy from Naples, Italy, in this way. The boy died about four hundred years ago. He must have come from a well-to-do family, because he was buried in an expensive coffin in an important church. When scientists uncovered his mummified body and saw his face, they suspected he died of smallpox. Pimplelike scars are typical of this very contagious disease.

Researchers soaked some of the scarred tissue in serum. Looking at it under a microscope, they saw evidence of the virus that causes smallpox. Without this microscopic evidence, they might have guessed why he died but would not have known for sure.

Along with studying tissues under a microscope, scientists sometimes do autopsies to examine mummies and other remains. An autopsy is a medical examination of a dead person. It involves cutting open the dead body and examining the organs and fluids within. In modern medicine, an autopsy is usually done to find out the cause of death, or occasionally to identify the person. With old or ancient remains, researchers look for much more than what killed a person.

The well-preserved bodies of Philip Calvert, his wife, and a baby were found in a Maryland cornfield in 1990.

Historians knew that Calvert was governor of the colony of Maryland in 1660 and 1661. The Calverts were well off for their time, but autopsies showed signs of a hard life.

The baby died of infection in the brain and spine. Governor Calvert had been in poor health. He died, possibly from a heart attack, at about age fifty. His wife died at about age fifty-five after much suffering. Her teeth and bones were in very poor condition, probably from lack of good nutrition. A broken leg had never healed and was infected. The Calvert mummies show that life in Colonial America, even for the well-to-do, was not easy.

Burial in a lead coffin preserved the bones, hair, and some of the soft tissue of this woman from Colonial Maryland. Since the carbon content of bones varies according to how much corn a person has eaten, scientists could tell that the woman was not born in the New World, where corn is commonly eaten, but had lived there for several years.

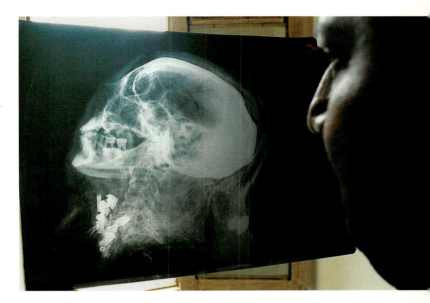

Top: *X rays of this Egyptian mummy's head revealed that eight of the man's molars were missing.*

TAKING PICTURES OF BONES

Autopsies and studies of tissue under a microscope can answer many questions about how and why people died in the past. But these methods involve cutting the dead body and removing tissue. X rays allow scientists to look inside bodies such as mummies without disturbing them.

X rays are helping scientists determine how the oldest known European died. In 1991, hikers came across a frozen body in the high Alps near the border between Austria and Italy. It is among the oldest and best-preserved mummies in the world.

The mummy is called the Iceman because his body was frozen for nearly five thousand years. He died in the mountains with no one to care for his dead body. A glacier covered him soon after death.

Right: *The oldest known European, known as the Iceman, lay undisturbed on a mountaintop for five thousand years until two hikers discovered his body in 1991.*

The Iceman brought many questions to scientists. Why did he die alone in the mountains? Where did he come from? Archaeologist Konrad Spindler headed the search to answer these questions. Spindler and other scientists looked at the Iceman's body, clothing, and the things he carried with him.

THE ICEMAN

By studying the body, scientists found that the Iceman had not been eating well. He had used up nearly all of his body fat. X rays showed broken ribs that had not healed. The Iceman had not been using his right arm for at least two or three weeks. Though the arm was not broken, scientists believe moving it made his ribs hurt.

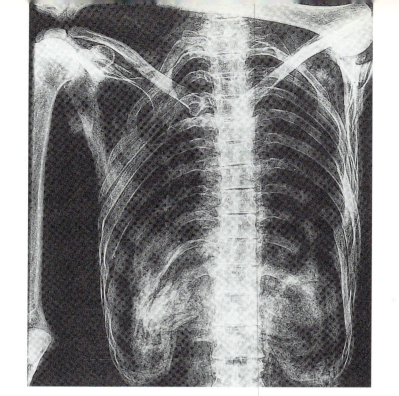

A possible cause of death for the Iceman emerged when scientists read his chest X rays (top). Broken ribs had not healed and may have made him unable to gather food. Hungry and cold in his grass cape (right), the Iceman became too weak to travel.

Among the things the Iceman carried were a copper ax with a wood handle, a flint knife in a case, an unfinished bow, and a quiver with two broken arrows and some unfinished arrows. The only food he had with him was a piece of dried meat and one small piece of fruit. Because this type of fruit does not ripen until late fall, scientists could pinpoint the time of year the Iceman had died. But this brought up more questions. Why did the Iceman go alone into the mountains with winter coming on? Why was his food almost gone?

Researchers found pieces of grain in the Iceman's clothes. This showed he had been below the mountain in fields planted with grain not long before his death. But his equipment was that of a mountain man, not a farmer. Maybe he was a shepherd who lived in a village below the mountain but spent much time herding sheep higher.

Why didn't the Iceman have a working bow and arrows? One clue came from the quiver. It was damaged and the cover was missing. Scientists think this may have happened when the two arrows were broken. They also believe the Iceman's bow broke at the same time. A used bowstring, perhaps from the broken bow, was in his backpack.

Top right: *Herders still bring their flocks high in the Alps where the Iceman was found.*
Above: *The Iceman's ax was perfectly preserved by the ice and snow that covered it.*

29

A VICTIM OF VIOLENCE

Piecing together these clues, Spindler and his team developed a theory about what happened to the Iceman. They believe he was a victim of violence. They think his broken ribs, damaged quiver, and broken bow and arrows all happened at the same time. Then he fled to the mountains where he tried to recover and repair his weapons.

To find out how long before death the violence occurred, Spindler consulted experimental archaeologists. Experimental archaeologists try to do everyday things people did in the past, exactly as they were done in the past. Spindler wanted to know how long it took the Iceman to cut down a tree with a copper ax and then carve the wood into a bow. Experimental archaeologist Harm Paulsen and others cut down trees with crude axes like the Iceman's, then carved bows from the wood, all in less than a day's time.

An experimental archaeologist starts a fire using the same simple tools people used thousands of years ago.

An artist trained in anthropology reconstructs the mummy's face, providing an intriguing view of the Iceman as he would have looked in life (inset).

But the Iceman was in pain. It must have taken him much longer to cut the wood and carve his bow. Without a bow, he was unable to hunt, which is probably why he was starving. Growing weaker from hunger and pain, he set down his ax, bow, and backpack. An early snowstorm came up. The Iceman probably knew how dangerous mountain snowstorms can be. Soon the cold overcame him and he lay down. He died as snow began to cover his body. The Iceman's body never thawed. A glacier covered it and did not melt until 1991.

GETTING THE COMPLETE PICTURE

While X rays and the work of experimental archaeologists can answer many questions, computers can take scientists a step farther. CT scanning uses computerized photography to show the inside of a body. CT is short for "computerized tomography." CT scans give a complete picture of a body without disturbing it from the outside. Scientists have used CT scans to study Egyptian mummies without cutting through the elaborate wrappings. Scans of a mummy from the Inca empire have uncovered a mystery surrounding how a young girl lived and died hundreds of years ago.

Five hundred years ago, much of Nevado Ampato, a volcano in Peru, was free of snow, allowing people to build a site for human sacrifice near the summit.

CHILDREN OF THE INCAS

More than five hundred years ago, the Incas were the largest and most powerful nation in North and South America. They lived in the Andes Mountains of western South America. Roads they constructed are still in use. They built huge, beautiful cities on the mountainsides.

Incas not only lived in the mountains, but also worshiped them as gods. They went to great lengths to build places of worship at the very tops of some of the highest mountains in the world.

Spanish priests wrote in the 1500s that the Incas sacrificed children to their mountain gods. One mountain they mentioned was Nevado Ampato, a volcano in Peru. In 1995, anthropologist Johan Reinhard climbed Ampato and discovered three mummies—two young children and a teenage girl. Their bodies had been frozen for five hundred years on the icy mountaintop.

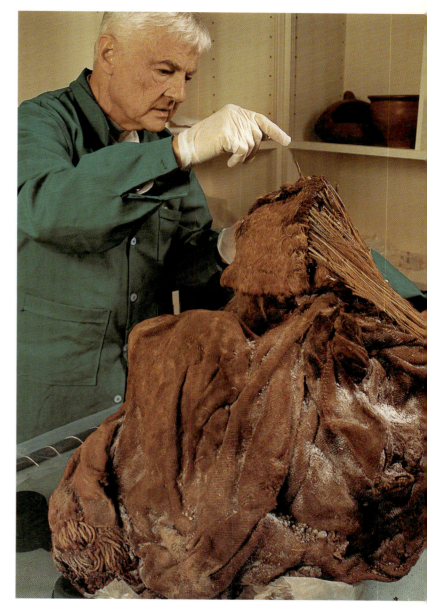

This mummified child was one of three found on Nevado Ampato by anthropologist Johan Reinhard.

The mummies wore beautifully woven clothing. They were buried with jewelry, statues, and decorated dishes. These artifacts all pointed to death by sacrifice, but there was no obvious evidence of violence. Reinhard thought the children probably died peacefully, by suffocation. He figured they were already exhausted from a two-day climb up the mountain. He guessed they were given an alcoholic drink to dull their minds and make them sleepy. Then it would have been easy for an adult to cover their faces until they stopped breathing.

The Inca chose the most perfect children to sacrifice to their mountain gods. This girl must have been beautiful in life.

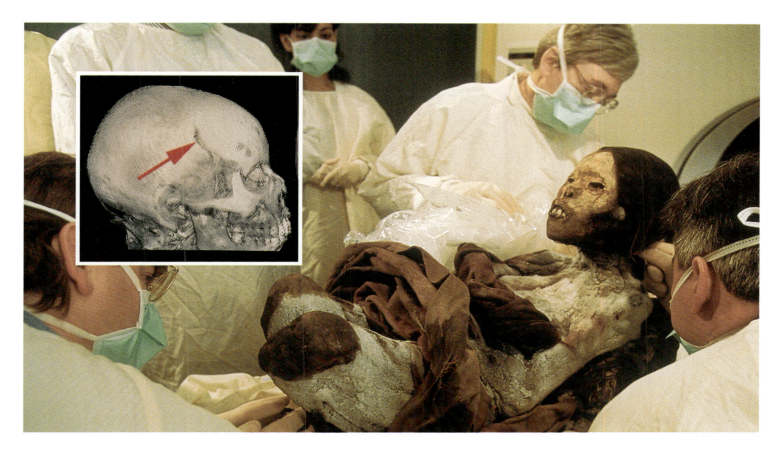

But CT scans of the teenage girl may tell another story. Her skull was broken and her brain was filled with blood from broken blood vessels. Some experts believe she was hit very hard on the head before her death. Other experts believe the skull was fractured later, after the girl died from the cold, still clutching her cloak in her fingers. We may never know what really happened.

Scientists ready the body of the Inca girl for scanning. CT scans (inset) of the girl's skull reveal a break that may have caused her death five hundred years ago.

An Old Disease in the New World

Most people die from natural causes or disease, not human sacrifice. Some South American mummies are helping scientists track one killer. Tuberculosis is a highly contagious disease that usually affects the lungs. It spreads from person to person by coughing and sneezing.

People in Europe, Asia, and Africa suffered from tuberculosis for thousands of years. Scientists once thought tuberculosis did not exist in North and South America until Europeans arrived there. But a thousand-year-old woman from Peru proved otherwise.

While examining the mummy of a woman in Peru, paleopathologist Arthur Aufderheide saw spots on her lungs that looked like tuberculosis. Aufderheide ordered a DNA profile of a sample of the lung tissue. This test looks at the codes carried on DNA molecules within the cells of living things. No one was sure if the test would work on mummified remains. The mummified lung tissue was very fragile. Still, scientists were able to find DNA from a bacterium that causes tuberculosis. This proved that tuberculosis was present in the Americas before Europeans arrived. By testing more mummies for tuberculosis, scientists can track how the disease spread in the past. This knowledge may help them learn how modern-day diseases spread.

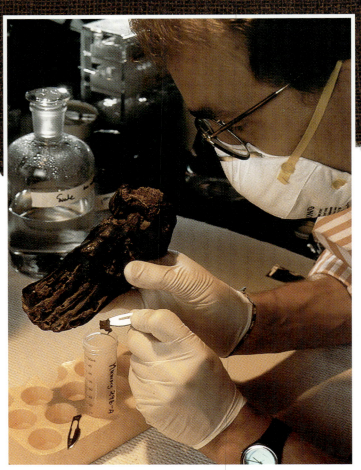

Above: *Mummified lung tissue from Peru helped scientists answer questions about tuberculosis, a highly deadly disease.*
Right: *A scientist removes a sample of tissue from an Egyptian mummy's foot for a DNA profile.*

Pathologist Johan Hultin crouches in the bottom of a mass grave in Brevig Mission, Alaska, where victims of the 1918 Spanish flu were buried and mummified in the frozen ground.

ON THE TRAIL OF A KILLER

Scientists hope a frozen mummy who died more than eighty years ago in Brevig Mission, Alaska, may keep us all safe from a killer flu. An especially deadly kind of influenza spread around the world in 1918 and 1919. Influenza, called flu for short, is a contagious disease similar to a bad cold with fever and muscle pains.

Influenza is usually mild and most people fight it off in a few days. But the 1918 flu, called the Spanish flu, turned deadly. It killed nearly a million people in North America and possibly more than forty million worldwide. When it hit Brevig Mission, most of the eighty people who lived there died.

Why did the Spanish flu become deadly in 1918? Could another fast-moving killer flu appear? If it did, could modern medicine save people from dying? Scientists have been trying to answer these questions since 1918.

In 1997, pathologist Johan Hultin went to Brevig Mission in search of tissue samples carrying the Spanish flu virus. The ground there is permanently frozen. Hultin dug up four bodies and found one of them well preserved. From the mummified body, Hultin was able to remove tissue samples containing the Spanish flu virus.

Hultin sent the samples to a research team in Washington, D.C. First the team studied the virus cells for information needed to make a vaccine, just in case the Spanish flu ever comes back. A vaccine is made from dead or weakened germs. The weakened germs are not strong enough to cause harm. They help the body recognize and fight off the disease later when stronger germs of the same kind attack.

The research team continues to study the Spanish flu cells to learn why the disease killed so many in 1918. If scientists can figure out what makes a usually mild disease turn deadly, they may be able to stop future outbreaks.

One flu victim, a woman, was well preserved. From her body (top)*, Hultin removed samples of lung tissue* (bottom) *for study.*

This body was buried and naturally mummified in the dry, hot sands near Arica, Chile.

Chapter 5

WHO WERE THEY?

For most people, seeing mummies brings questions to mind. Even after we know when and how people died, we wonder about them. Who were they? Where did they come from? How did they live? Scientists ask these questions too, of mummies and bones and body parts.

When many mummies are buried together over time, scientists can piece together the history of a people even when no written records exist. One of the best places for this type of work is a stretch of desert coastline along the Pacific Ocean in South America. It is the driest place on earth. Bodies buried in the hot sand dry out quickly, often becoming mummies.

People called the Chinchorro buried their dead on these beaches for thousands of years, until about 1500 B.C. Scientists named the people after Chinchorro Beach in Arica, Chile, where some of their dead were found. No one knows what the Chinchorro called themselves. They left no written records. But they left thousands of mummies to tell their story.

This young boy was mummified and his face covered with a paste mask according to the traditions of the Chinchorro, who lived in Chile thousands of years ago.

STORIES STORED INSIDE

The Chinchorro were one of the earliest peoples to practice embalming. Preserving the dead must have been very important to them. They took great pains to embalm bodies. They used an elaborate process that began with removing the skin and muscles.

The skeleton was taken apart and cleaned. Then it was put back together by tying it onto a wooden framework. Next, embalmers covered everything with a body cast made of mud or paste, shaping the face into a mask. Finally the whole thing was painted.

The goal of Chinchorro embalming seems to have been to create a statue out of the dead person. Scientists think the Chinchorro did not bury the bodies right away. Some of the mummies were repainted before burial.

Researchers think they may have been kept in the family home or put on display before being buried.

The Chinchorro bodies have many stories to tell. By examining their bones and intestines, scientists learned the Chinchorro got most of their food from the sea. Sea lion meat, fish, shellfish, and seaweed provided good nutrition.

The bodies of Chinchorro men and women showed some differences. Many of the men had growths in their ears caused by spending much time in cold water. This shows that the men probably did most of the fishing and diving for shellfish and seaweed. Many men, but none of the women, had small breaks in bones of their lower backs. These probably happened from falling on slippery rocks along the shore.

Chinchorro women suffered from a different back problem. Their bones were not healthy, probably because they did not have enough calcium in their diet during pregnancy and nursing.

Some researchers think Chinchorro beliefs about caring for the dead may have been responsible for another health problem. Nearly half the Chinchorro mummies studied had serious infections on their legs. Scientists believe these infections could have been caused by constant contact with dead bodies.

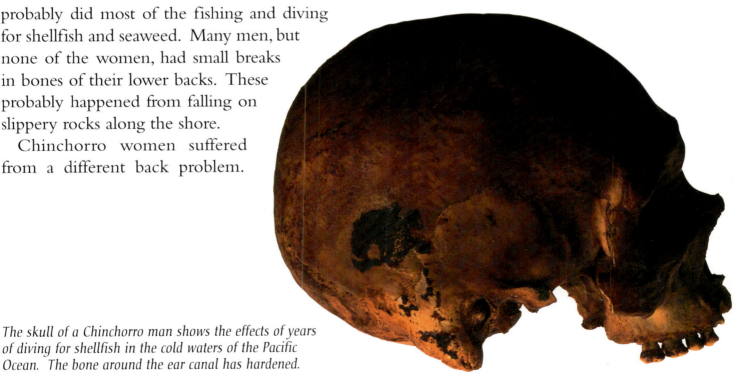

The skull of a Chinchorro man shows the effects of years of diving for shellfish in the cold waters of the Pacific Ocean. The bone around the ear canal has hardened.

AN OASIS FULL OF MUMMIES

The ways in which people care for the dead change over time, even in a place like Egypt with its world-famous mummies and tombs. One day in 1996, an Egyptian man was riding his donkey to work at a temple in the Bahariya Oasis in central Egypt. As the man's donkey walked along the path, its foot fell into a hole. The man looked into the hole and saw gold-covered mummies lying side by side. Until that day, no one knew they were there.

Egyptian scientists rushed to Bahariya Oasis to investigate. After months of work, they located about 150 underground tombs, containing thousands of mummies. More tombs may yet be discovered.

A stumbling donkey helped uncover tombs filled with mummies at the Bahariya Oasis in central Egypt. Settlements there date back 2,300 years. Archaeologists believe that people living at the Bahariya Oasis in ancient times became wealthy growing grapes for making wine.

A SPECIAL KIND OF MUMMY

Who were the people buried in these tombs? The Bahariya Oasis mummies are different from most other Egyptian mummies. They are people who lived during the time when Greece and Rome controlled Egypt (from 332 B.C. to about A.D. 350). Most Egyptian mummies are older, dating from the time when Egyptians ruled their own land.

When Greece and Rome conquered Egypt, they brought European beliefs and traditions. The people of the Bahariya Oasis mixed these foreign beliefs with their ancient Egyptian traditions. Burial masks on the Bahariya Oasis mummies show Greek-style portraits with European hairdos. Paintings of Greek, Roman, and Egyptian gods decorate the mummy wrappings. Many mummies were not buried in traditional Egyptian coffins but were simply wrapped and placed in tombs.

These mummies are important to scientists for another reason. At the Bahariya Oasis, people lived and buried their dead in the same place for more than six hundred years. Whole families are buried together, sometimes for several generations. The Bahariya Oasis mummies can help scientists track how peoples' lives changed over the centuries. Their story will unfold for years to come as scientists continue to study them.

Further study of decorative coffins, some covered with gold, will provide clues about how Greek and Roman traditions mixed with traditional Egyptian beliefs in the years when Greece and Rome ruled Egypt.

Wisps of light-colored hair escape from the woolen headwrap worn by this mummified infant from Xinjiang, China. Soft stones cover the baby's eyes.

EUROPEANS IN ANCIENT CHINA

Human remains can also help scientists piece together where people came from in the ancient past. Mummies found in the province of Xinjiang in northwestern China surprised many scientists. The mummies are three to four thousand years old, preserved by the desert climate in which they were buried.

What is surprising about these mummies is that they have light skin and European-looking features. Many have light-colored hair. People with these traits are called Caucasian. More than one hundred Caucasian bodies have been discovered in China. All were found along China's Silk Road. The Silk Road carried traders from the West into China to buy silk, tea, and other goods.

Historians knew that Caucasian people traveled to China in the ancient past. But until recently most scientists did not think they lived in China. The large number of Caucasian mummies in Xinjiang, home to the Uygur people, proved that idea wrong.

Human remains can link modern-day people with ancient groups. Some groups, including the Uygur of Xinjiang, appreciate knowing more about their ancestors. But discoveries of human remains can sometimes bring more questions than answers. They add fuel to the debate about whether it is right to dig up the dead and study their bones.

Modern-day residents of Xinjiang, China, were so taken by the beauty of this Caucasian mummy (above) *that they wrote a song in her honor* (right).

The Uygur people of modern Xinjiang look more Caucasian than Chinese. They speak their own language and have their own form of writing. The Chinese government wants the Uygur to adopt Chinese ways, but they have resisted. The discovery of Caucasian mummies has only added to the tension.

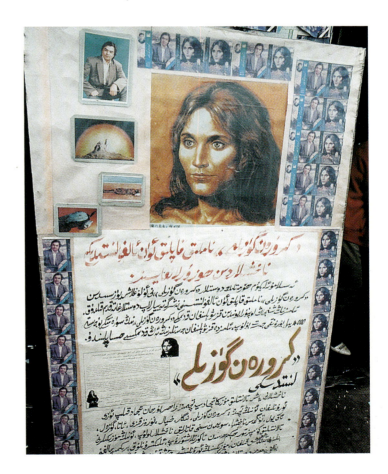

In the late 1800s, adventurers such as Earl Morris (above, left) combed the American Southwest looking for ancient remains, pottery, tools, and baskets. Modern-day archaeologists in Asia unearthed these skulls (opposite) for study.

WHAT TO DO WITH MUMMIES AND BONES

People long ago probably never imagined that their bodies might be uncovered after burial. They probably never thought that scientists would study their tissue under a microscope, or that grave robbers might disturb their bones. But dead bodies and body parts have been handled—and mishandled—over the centuries. How to treat human remains continues to be an important question all over the world.

In North America, it is illegal for people to keep human remains they find. Often remains are turned over to the police, to doctors, or to the government. Experts try to identify the body and find living relatives whenever possible. Those relatives are usually allowed to rebury the body or bones as long as they are not needed to solve a crime.

Identifying Human Remains

Twenty-five years after the end of the Vietnam War, the remains of U.S. soldiers are still being returned. When the Vietnamese government turns a body or bones over to the Americans, often no one knows who it is. The remains are placed in a coffin and draped with an American flag. They are then flown to the U.S. Army Central Identification Laboratory in Hawaii.

When the plane lands in Hawaii, it is met by an honor guard of soldiers from every branch of the military in dress uniforms. The reason for this is that no one knows in which branch the dead person served. The honor guard marches into the airplane and carries the coffin to the laboratory.

Inside the laboratory, scientists study the remains. No one may enter the room without permission, and all who enter must remove their hats in honor of the dead. All remains are covered with white sheets when they are not being examined. In the evening, all sheets are neatly folded once again to cover every set of remains, even the smallest pile of bones.

When a set of remains is identified, it is once again placed in a coffin and covered with an American flag. Another honor guard, this time from the branch of the military in which the dead person served, carries the coffin to an airplane. It is then flown to the soldier's family.

The body of an American serviceman, First Lieutenant Michael Blassie, was buried in 1998. Killed during the Vietnam War in 1972, his remains were positively identified using DNA testing.

LEAVING BONES ALONE

When no living relatives are found, it's harder to know what to do with old bones. Should they be put on display? Should scientists be able to study them? A growing number of people believe scientists should leave dead bodies alone.

Some Native Americans have gone to court to force scientists to hand over skeletons. They have then reburied the remains with religious ceremonies.

Called the Indian Burial Pit by its owners, this Native American burial place (left) near Salina, Kansas, was operated as a tourist attraction beginning in the 1930s. Pawnee and other Indians successfully fought for the right to close the attraction and rebury their ancestors (above) in 1990.

In 1990, the U.S. Congress passed the Native American Graves Protection and Repatriation Act. This act gives Native Americans control over all native remains buried on government lands or held in collections owned or funded by the government. The same act makes it illegal for anyone to sell native dead bodies. Many native skeletons and mummies are still stored in schools and private collections across the country, but Native American groups are working to change this.

Anthropologists hired by museums (above and right) work to identify Native American remains and return them to their relatives for reburial.

King Ramses II rests in the Royal Mummies Room at the Egyptian Museum in Cairo in a case designed to protect his remains from decay and damage.

A NEW HOME FOR EGYPT'S KINGS

People in other parts of the world are also trying to preserve the dignity of human remains. Anwar Sadat, former president of Egypt, was saddened by the way the ancient kings of Egypt were displayed at the Egyptian Museum in Cairo, Egypt. The museum was old and rundown. Some of the mummies were not well cared for. In 1979, Sadat ordered the royal mummy display shut down. He did not think it was worthy of the mummies' noble ranks.

The museum spent many years giving the royal mummies a new home called the Royal Mummies Room. This room has special cases that protect the mummies from decay and damage. Visitors are not allowed to talk when they tour the room, in honor of the dead. The Egyptian government hopes their new mummy room will encourage other museums to show more respect for dead bodies on display.

MUMMIES AND BONES FOR SALE

Over the years, people have tried to profit from human bodies and burial grounds. Grave robbers have been at work since the days of ancient Egypt. In North and South America, people continue to dig up Native American graves because they know collectors will pay high prices for the artifacts. Many times the bones are simply left scattered on the ground.

Sometimes people turn the dead into sideshow attractions. A store in Seattle, Washington, has human mummies on display for customers to look at while they shop. The mummies are more than one hundred years old. One was found shot to death in the Arizona desert and was naturally mummified. Another was from Central America. They ended up as store props because no one knew who they were and no one thought to bury them.

Sylvester, as his owners call him, greets customers at Ye Olde Curiosity Shop in Seattle, Washington.

Elmer McCurdy was put on display for sixty-five years before he was finally buried. McCurdy was a train robber who was shot in Oklahoma in 1911. His body was taken to the local funeral parlor. When the funeral director learned that McCurdy had no family to pay for embalming, he decided to let McCurdy pay for it himself. The funeral director embalmed McCurdy with extra-strong materials. Then he charged people money to see the outlaw.

One day a visitor told the funeral director that McCurdy was his brother and he wanted to bury him. The funeral director gave the man the body, but it was not buried. The man was not McCurdy's brother, but a carnival operator. McCurdy spent the next fifty years or more traveling in carnival sideshows.

In 1976, the crew of *The Six-Million Dollar Man* television show went to an amusement park to film a scene. The plot involved a chase through a house of horrors. When a crew member picked up what he thought was a fake dead man, an arm fell off. A human bone was clearly seen, and the police were called. When the body was identified as McCurdy's, it was finally claimed and sent to Oklahoma to be buried, sixty-five years late.

Elmer McCurdy's burial was postponed by sixty-five years, as people profited from the display of his mummified body.

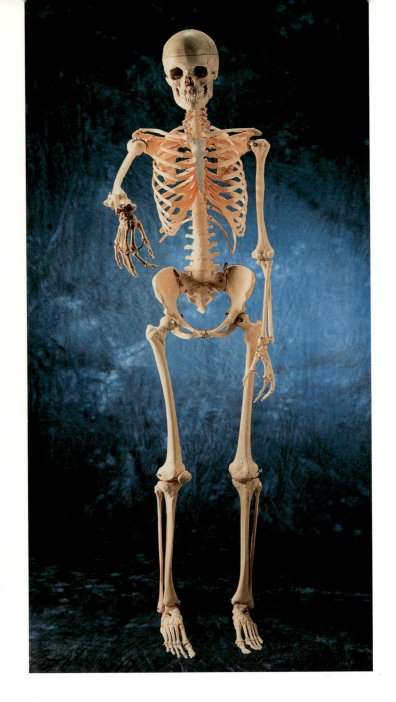

BODIES AND PARTS FOR SALE

For several hundred years, well-preserved bodies and body parts have been used in medical schools. The body parts give students a firsthand look inside the human body. In times gone by, teachers in medical schools earned money by selling tickets to their classes. They always wanted to have the most eye-catching dead bodies. The more students who took their classes, the more money they made.

Modern medical schools use dead bodies just for study, not for making money. Some of these bodies are donated by people before death. Others are bodies of people who had no relatives to claim them for burial. Many classrooms have real skeletons on display to teach about the human body. But the best specimens are those with soft tissues.

Many people donate their bodies to science so that, after death, their organs can help those awaiting transplants or their skeletons can help students learning about human anatomy.

One way of preserving soft tissues is called plastination. It makes modern mummies that help doctors learn surgery and other skills. Plastination was developed in Germany about twenty years ago. Tissues are freeze-dried to remove all water. Then the water is replaced with plastic. The process takes several months. The result is a very lifelike specimen that keeps the color and shape of living tissue. Plastination is mostly performed on parts of bodies, although whole bodies have also been treated in this way. It is accepted worldwide as the best way to preserve human body tissue for teaching medical students.

This human head was preserved by a process called plastination. Plastinated organs, limbs, and whole bodies provide lifelike specimens for medical students.

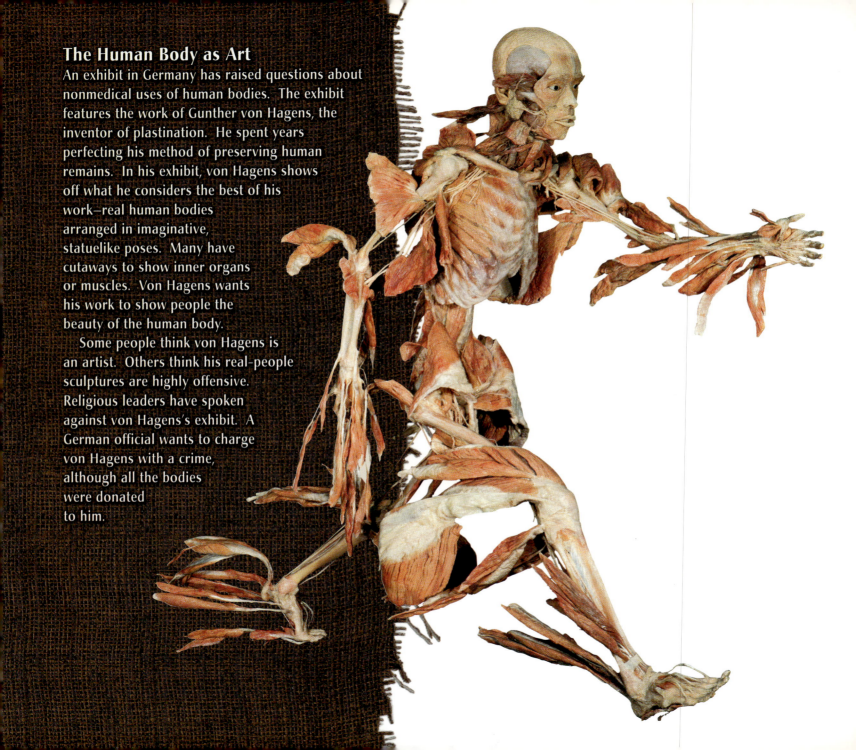

The Human Body as Art

An exhibit in Germany has raised questions about nonmedical uses of human bodies. The exhibit features the work of Gunther von Hagens, the inventor of plastination. He spent years perfecting his method of preserving human remains. In his exhibit, von Hagens shows off what he considers the best of his work—real human bodies arranged in imaginative, statuelike poses. Many have cutaways to show inner organs or muscles. Von Hagens wants his work to show people the beauty of the human body.

Some people think von Hagens is an artist. Others think his real-people sculptures are highly offensive. Religious leaders have spoken against von Hagens's exhibit. A German official wants to charge von Hagens with a crime, although all the bodies were donated to him.

PUTTING THE DEAD TO REST

In recent years, there has been great interest in studying dead bodies. New technology allows scientists to learn much more from human remains than they could in the past. More efforts are being made than ever before to study mummies, bones, and body parts. This bothers people who believe respect for the dead is more important than what can be learned by digging up remains.

But in some cases, scientists rescue ancient bodies from a worse fate, grave robbing. This is a serious problem, even in the most out-of-the-way places. Grave robbers often destroy bodies and bones or leave them scattered out in the open.

If scientists had not dug up the Pazyryk lady, would she still be resting peacefully in her mountain grave? Or would robbers have found her gold and treasures by now, leaving her body to decay in the sun?

No one can make certain that every dead body will rest quietly in the earth. But scientists and religious and cultural leaders are beginning to work together to make sure all human remains are treated with the respect their families wanted them to have.

This person died thousands of years ago in Peru but will no longer enjoy a quiet rest. The mummy and clothes will be preserved for study, allowing scientists to learn more about our human past.

GLOSSARY

archaeologist: a scientist who investigates the past by studying artifacts, buildings, ancient writing, and other objects

autopsy: an examination performed on a dead person, usually to find the cause of death

bacteria: microscopic living things that exist almost everywhere. Many bacteria are useful, but some cause disease.

cryonics: the practice of freezing the body of a person who dies, in hopes of bringing the person back to life at a future time

CT scan: sometimes called CAT scan, short for computerized axial tomography. This special kind of X ray uses computerized photography to show the inside of a body.

DNA: short for deoxyribonucleic acid, the molecule carrying the information or special codes that give each living thing its unique characteristics

DNA profile: a laboratory test that analyzes the codes carried on DNA molecules

embalming: treating a dead body in order to preserve it from decay

experimental archaeologist: a person trained and skilled in trying to duplicate everyday things people did in the past, exactly as they were done in the past

forensic anthropologist: a scientist who studies human remains for the purpose of solving crimes or settling disputes in court

mummification: the process of turning a dead body into a mummy. Mummification occurs naturally, as when a body is quickly dried or frozen, or by embalming.

mummy: a body in which the soft tissues did not decay after death

paleopathologist: a scientist who studies ancient human remains, especially preserved soft tissues

physical anthropologist: a scientist who studies human remains for the purpose of learning about human history

plastination: a method of preserving body tissue by replacing the water in it with plastic

radiocarbon dating: estimating the age of old material by measuring how much of a certain type of carbon atom it contains

rehydration: the process of putting water back into tissues that once were moist but have dried out

remains: a dead body or parts of something that was once alive

soft tissue: skin, muscles, and organs

vaccine: a substance containing dead, weakened, or living organisms that can be injected or taken orally. The vaccine causes a person to produce antibodies that protect against the disease caused by the organisms.

X ray: a photograph made by a special camera that uses invisible, high-energy beams of light that can pass through solid objects

When people bury their loved ones, they rarely imagine that others may uncover the remains years later. Here archaeologists uncover mummies in an Egyptian tomb.

SELECTED BIBLIOGRAPHY

Allen, Thomas B. "The Silk Road's Lost World." *National Geographic* (March 1996): 44–51.

Arriaza, Bernardo. "Chile's Chinchorro Mummies." *National Geographic* (March 1995): 68–89.

Aufderheide, Arthur C., and Conrado Rodrìguez–Martin. *The Cambridge Encyclopedia of Human Paleopathology.* Cambridge, England: Cambridge University Press, 1998.

Brier, Bob. *The Encyclopedia of Mummies.* New York: Checkmark Books, 1998.

Christensen, D. "Pre-Columbian Mummies Lay TB Debate to Rest." *Science News* (March 19, 1994):181.

Franklin–Barbajosa, Cassandra. "The New Face of Identity." *National Geographic* (May 1992): 112–124.

Hadingham, Evan. "The Mummies of Xinjiang." *Discover* (April 1994): 68–77.

Hawass, Zahi. "Oasis of the Dead." *Archaeology* (September/October 1999): 38–43.

Larson, Erik. "The Flu Hunters." *Time* (February 23, 1998): 53–64.

Maples, William R., and Michael Browning. *Dead Men Do Tell Tales.* New York: Doubleday, 1994.

Polosmak, Natalya. "A Mummy Unearthed from the Pastures of Heaven." *National Geographic* (October 1994): 80–103.

Reinhard, Johan. "Peru's Ice Maidens." *National Geographic* (June 1996): 62–81.

Reinhard, Johan. "Sacred Peaks of the Andes." *National Geographic* (March 1992): 84–111.

Reinhard, Johan. "Sharp Eyes of Science Probe the Mummies of Peru." *National Geographic* (January 1997): 36–43.

Roberts, David. "The Iceman." *National Geographic* (June 1993): 36–67.

Spindler, Konrad, et al. *Human Mummies.* New York: Springer-Verlag Wien, 1996.

"Tales from the Crypt." *Time* (April 18, 1994): 67.

Toufexis, Anastasia. "The Mummy's Tale." *Time* (March 28, 1994): 53.

Turner, R. C., and R. G. Scaife. *Bog Bodies: New Discoveries and New Perspectives.* London: British Museum Press, 1995.

Webster, Donovan. "Valley of the Mummies." *National Geographic* (October 1999): 76–87.

Weeks, Kent R. "Valley of the Kings." *National Geographic* (September 1998): 2–33.

RESOURCES ON MUMMIES

For Further Reading

Deem, James M. *Bodies from the Bog*. Boston: Houghton Mifflin Company, 1998. Deem explores the lives and deaths of people whose bodies have been preserved for hundreds of years in peat bogs throughout Europe.

Deem, James M. Illustrated by True Kelley. *How to Make a Mummy Talk*. Boston: Houghton Mifflin Company, 1995. Deem explores all kinds of myths surrounding mummies.

Echo-Hawk, Roger C. and Walter R. Echo-Hawk. *Battlefields and Burial Grounds: The Indian Struggle to Protect Ancestral Graves in the United States*. Minneapolis, MN: Lerner Publications Company, 1994. The authors look at the treatment of Native American remains and efforts to return remains to living relatives.

Getz, David. *Frozen Girl*. New York: Henry Holt and Company, 1998. In this chapter book, Getz uses interviews with scientists to tell the story of the young Inca girl whose mummified body was found in Peru by anthropologist Johan Reinhard.

Jackson, Donna M. *The Bone Detectives: How Forensic Anthropologists Solve Crimes and Uncover Mysteries of the Dead*. Boston: Little, Brown and Company, 1995. Illustrated with many photographs, this book tells the story of scientists who study bones, hair, teeth, and other human remains to find missing persons and solve crimes.

Quinlan, Susan E. *The Case of the Mummified Pigs and Other Mysteries in Nature*. Honesdale, PA: Boyds Mills Press, 1995. In the title essay in this collection, Quinlan explains how, by experimenting with dead piglets, one scientist helped determine why most bodies decompose, but others become mummies.

Reinhard, Johan. *Discovering the Inca Ice Maiden: My Adventures on Ampato*. Washington, DC: National Geographic Society, 1998. In words and photographs, Dr. Reinhard, an anthropologist, recounts his discovery of the mummified body of a young girl from the time of the Incas.

Wilcox, Charlotte. *Mummies & Their Mysteries*. Minneapolis, MN: Carolrhoda Books, Inc., 1993. Using many photographs to illustrate her points, Wilcox outlines the different kinds of mummies found around the world and explains how they are made or how they occur naturally.

Websites

For a wealth of information on mummies, search for the word mummies at
   http://www.pbs.org/wgbh/nova/search.html
For information on cryonic storage, see
   http://www.cryonics.org
For information on bog bodies, see
   http://uts.cc.utexas.edu/~dente/bogbodies.htm
For information on Canada's Iceman from the 1450s, see
   http://www.archaeology.org/online/news/iceman
For an interactive journey with anthropologist Johan Reinhard, see
   http://www.nationalgeographic.com/mummy/index.html
For information on efforts to return Native American remains to living relatives, see
   http://www.nmnh.si.edu/anthro/repatriation/
For a review of Gunther von Hagens's plastinated human sculptures, see
   http://www.shul.org/corpse.htm

INDEX

References to captions appear in italics.

ACKNOWLEDGEMENTS

The photographs in this book are reproduced through the courtesy of: The National Museum of Denmark, pp. 1, 24; © Stephen Alvarez, pp. 2, 32, 33, 34; © Eric Brissaud/Liaison Agency, pp. 5, 13; Laura Westlund, p. 6; © Charles O'Rear/Corbis, pp. 7, 8, 9; © Nicole Thompson, p. 10; © Corbis/Bettmann-UPI, p. 11; © Kenneth Garrett, pp. 12, 15, 17, 27 (top), 28 (bottom), 29 (both), 30, 31 (both), 42, 43, 51, 59, 64; Cryonics Institute, p. 14; © Marc Deville/Liaison Agency, pp. 16, 57; © National Museum of Ireland, p. 18; Sam Vastro, Radiocarbon Laboratory, University of Texas at Austin, p. 19; Cheshire County Constabulary, p. 20; The British Museum, pp. 21, 22; © Sarah Gaunt/Champagne and Aishihik First Nations, p. 23; G. Fornaciari and L. Capasso, p. 25 (left); Dr. A. C. Aufderheide, University of Minnesota, Duluth, pp. 25 (right), 36 (left); Markus White/Historic St. Mary's City Commission, p. 26; © Paul Hanny/Liaison Agency, p. 27 (bottom); Dieter zur Nedden, p. 28 (top); © Maria Stenzel/National Geographic Image Collection, p. 35; Dr. Elliot Fishman, Johns Hopkins Hospital, p. 35 (inset); © Peter Menzel, p. 36 (right); Johan V. Hultin, pp. 37, 38 (both); © Enrico Ferorelli, pp. 39, 40, 41; Jeffery Newbury/©1994. Reprinted with permission of Discover Magazine, p. 44; © Reza Deghati/National Geographic Image Collection, p. 45 (both); Neg. no. 127468, photo by E. H. Morris, courtesy Department of Library Services, American Museum of Natural History, p. 46; Liaison Agency, p. 47; Sgt. Scott Seyer/Air Force News Agency/www.af.mil/news, p. 48; Kansas State Historical Society, p. 49 (bottom left); Scott Williams, The Salina Journal, p. 49 (top right); David R. Hunt, Anthropology, National Museum of Natural History, Smithsonian Institution, p. 50 (both); Ye Olde Curiosity Shop, p. 52; Western History Collections, University of Oklahoma Libraries, p. 53; Institut fur Plastination, Heidelberg, Germany, pp. 54, 55, 56.

Front cover: © Stephen Alvarez
Back cover: © Kenneth Garrett
Designed by Michael Tacheny

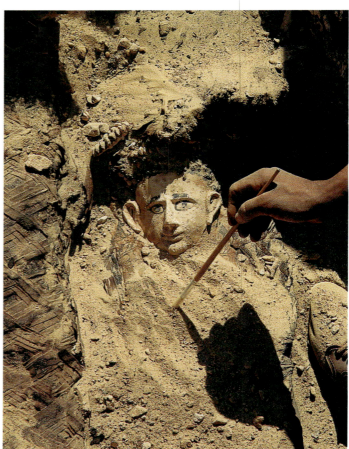

An archaeologist dusts off the face mask of the mummy of an Egyptian child buried at the Bahariya Oasis.